CITY NOISE

by Karla Kuskin · illustrated by Renée Flower

HarperCollins*Publishers*

For Maddie and Jake, the new noisemakers
—K. K.

In memory of my mother,
whose love still shelters her little wren
—R. F.

So what did you see?

**An old tin can,
It was sitting in the gutter
I took it in my hand.**

**I held it very carefully against my ear
And listened, listened, listened.**

So what did you hear?

**Squalling
Calling**

**Crashing
Rushing**

**Honking
Joking**

**Belching
Smoking**

**Buying
Selling**

**Laughing
Yelling**

**Running
Wheeling**

**Roaring
Squealing**

Cars and garbage

Reds and greens

Girls and women

Men

Machines

Getting
Giving

Dogs and boys

Living

Living

Living

ity noise.

Library of Congress Cataloging-in-Publication Data Kuskin, Karla. City Noise / by Karla Kuskin; illustrated by Renée Flower. p. cm. Summary: In this poem, an old tin can becomes an urban conch shell when, held against a child's ear, it reveals the sounds of a bustling city. ISBN 0-06-021076-1. —ISBN 0-06-021077-X (lib. bdg.) 1. City and town life—Juvenile poetry. 2. Children's poetry, American. [1. City and town life—Poetry. 2. Sound—Poetry. 3. Noise—Poetry. 4. American Poetry.] I. Flower, Renée, ill. II. Title. PS3561.U79C57 1994 91-44213 811'.54—dc20 CIP AC 1 2 3 4 5 6 7 8 9 10 ❖ First Edition